Janice VanCleave's
MAGNETS

JANICE VANCLEAVE'S
SPECTACULAR SCIENCE PROJECTS

Animals
Earthquakes
Gravity
Machines
Magnets
Molecules

JANICE VANCLEAVE'S
SCIENCE FOR EVERY KID SERIES

Astronomy for Every Kid
Biology for Every Kid
Chemistry for Every Kid
Earth Science for Every Kid
Math for Every Kid
Physics for Every Kid

Spectacular Science Projects

Janice VanCleave's
MAGNETS

Mind-boggling Experiments You Can Turn Into Science Fair Projects

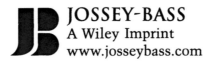

JOSSEY-BASS
A Wiley Imprint
www.josseybass.com

Published by Jossey-Bass
A Wiley Imprint
989 Market Street, San Francisco, CA 94103-1741   www.josseybass.com

Published simultaneously in Canada.

Design and Production by Navta Associates, Inc.
Illustrated by Doris Ettlinger.

Jossey-Bass books and products are available through most bookstores. To contact Jossey-Bass directly call our Customer Care Department within the U.S. at 800-956-7739, outside the U.S. at 317-572-3986, or fax 317-572-4002.

Jossey-Bass also publishes its books in a variety of electronic formats. Some content that appears in print may not be available in electronic books.

Library of Congress Cataloging-in-Publication Data

VanCleave, Janice Pratt.
  [Magnets]
  Janice VanCleave's magnets.
  p. cm. — (Spectacular Science Projects)
  Includes index.
  Summary: A collection of science projects and experiments using magnets.
  ISBN 0-471-57106-7 (pbk.)
  1. Magnets—Experiments—Juvenile literature. 2. Science projects—Juvenile literature. 3. Science—Exhibitions—Juvenile literature. [1. Magnets—Experiments. 2. Experiments. 3. Science projects.] I. Title. II. Title: Magnets. III. Series: VanCleave, Janice Pratt. Janice VanCleave's spectacular science projects.
  QC753.7.V35   1993
  538 '.4078—dc20   92-21348

FIRST EDITION
PB Printing   20 19 18 17 16 15 14 13 12 11

CONTENTS

Dedicated to a very special friend, my sister,
Dianne Pratt Fleming

Introduction

Science is a search for answers. Science projects are good ways to learn more about science as you search for the answers to specific problems. This book will give you guidance and provide ideas, but you must do your part in the search by planning experiments, finding and recording information related to the problem, and organizing the data collected to find the answer to the problem. Sharing your findings by presenting your project at science fairs will be a rewarding experience if you have properly prepared for the exhibit. Trying to assemble a project overnight results in frustration, and you cheat yourself out of the fun of being a science detective. Solving a scientific mystery, like solving a detective mystery, requires planning and the careful collecting of facts. The following sections provide suggestions for how to get started on this scientific quest. Start the project with curiosity and a desire to learn something new.

SELECT A TOPIC

The 20 topics in this book suggest many possible problems to solve. Each topic has one "cookbook" experiment—follow the recipe and the result is guaranteed. Approximate metric equivalents have been given after all English measurements. Try several or all of these easy experiments before choosing the topic you like best and want to know more about. Regardless of the problem you choose to solve, what you discover will make you more knowledgeable about magnets.

KEEP A JOURNAL

Purchase a bound notebook in which you will write everything relating to the project. This is your journal. It will contain your original ideas as well as ideas you get from books or from people like teachers and scientists. It will include descriptions of your experiments as well as diagrams, photographs, and written observations of all your results. Every entry should be as neat as possible and dated. Information from this journal can be used to write a report of your project, and you will want to display the journal with your completed project. A neat, orderly journal provides a complete and accurate record of your project from start to finish. It is also proof of the time you spent sleuthing out the answers to the scientific mystery you undertook to solve.

LET'S EXPLORE

This section of each chapter follows each of the 20 sample experiments and provides additional questions about the problem presented in the experiment. By making small changes to some part of the sample experiment, new results are achieved. Think about why these new results might have happened.

SHOW TIME!

You can use the pattern of the sample experiment to design your own experiments to solve the questions asked in "Let's Explore." Your own experiment should follow the sample experiment's format and include a single question about one idea, a list of necessary materials, a detailed step-by-step procedure, written results with diagrams, graphs, and charts if they seem helpful, and a conclusion answering the question and explaining your answer. Include any information you found through research to clarify your answer. When you design your own experiments, make sure to get adult approval if supplies or procedures other than those given in this book are used.

If you want to make a science fair project, study the information listed here and after each sample experiment in the book to develop your ideas into a real science fair exhibit. Use the suggestions that best apply to the project topic that you have chosen. Keep in mind that while your display represents all the work that you have done, it must tell the story of the project in such a way that it attracts and holds the interest of the viewer. So keep it simple. Do not try to cram all of your information into one place. To have more space on the display and still exhibit all your work, keep some of the charts, graphs, pictures, and other materials in your journal instead of on the display board itself.

The actual size and shape of displays can be different, depending on the local science fair officials, so you will have to check the rules for your science fair. Most exhibits are allowed to be 48 inches (122 cm) wide, 30 inches (76 cm) deep, and 108 inches (274 cm) high. These are maximum measurements and your display may be smaller than this. A three-sided backboard (see drawing) is usually the best way to display your work. Wooden panels can be hinged together, but you can also use sturdy cardboard pieces taped together to form a very inexpensive but presentable exhibit.

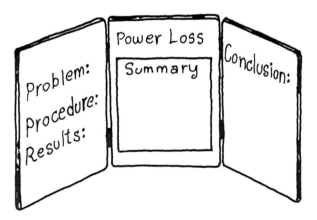

A good title of six words or less with a maximum of 50 characters should be placed at the top of the center panel. The title should capture the theme of the project but should not be the same as the problem statement. For example, if the problem under question is *Can magnets be demagnetized?*, a good title for the project may be "Power Loss." The title and other headings should be neat and large enough to be readable at a distance of about 3 feet (1 meter). You can glue letters to the backboard (you can use precut letters that you buy or letters that you cut out of construction paper), or you can stencil the letters for all the titles. A short summary paragraph of about 100 words to explain the scientific principles involved is good and can be printed under the title. A person who has no knowledge of the topic should be able to easily understand the basic idea of the project just from reading the summary.

There are no set rules about the position of the information on the display. However, it all needs to be well organized, with the title and summary paragraph as the main point at the top of the center panel and the remaining material placed neatly from left to right under specific headings. Choices of headings will depend on how you wish to display the information. Separate headings for Problem, Procedure, Results, and Conclusion may be used.

The judges give points for how clearly you are able to discuss the project and explain its purpose, procedure, results, and conclusion. The display should be organized so that it explains everything, but your ability to discuss your project and answer the questions of the judges convinces them that you did the work and understand what you have done. Practice a speech in front of friends, and invite them to ask you questions. If you do not know the answer to a question, never guess or make up an answer or just say, "I do not know." Instead, you can say that you did not discover that answer during your research and then offer other information that you found of interest about the project. Be proud of the project and approach the judges with enthusiasm about your work.

CHECK IT OUT!

Read about your topic in many books and magazines. You are more likely to have a successful project if you are well informed about the topic. For the topics in this book, some tips are provided about specific places to look for information. Record in your journal all the information you find, and include for each source the author's name, the book title (or magazine name and article title), the numbers of the pages you read, the publisher's name, where it was published, and the year of publication.

1

Stickers

PROBLEM

What materials are attracted to a magnet?

Materials

testing materials: aluminum foil, copper wire, glass marble, iron nail, paper, steel BBs, wooden match

bar magnet

Procedure

1. Lay the testing materials on a *wooden* table.

2. Touch the magnet to, and slowly move the magnet away from, each material.

3. Observe and record which materials cling to the magnet.

Results

The iron nail and the BBs are the only materials that cling to the magnet.

Why?

All materials, including the testing materials, are made up of tiny bits of matter called **atoms**. For example, the smallest part of an iron nail is an atom of iron, and the smallest part of a glass marble is an atom of glass. Materials are **magnetic** because of the way their atoms group together.

When clusters of atoms organize themselves, the atoms are attracted to different areas of the earth's magnetic field. One side of the cluster is attracted to the earth's magnetic **north pole** and the

other side is attracted to the earth's magnetic **south pole**. These clusters of atoms are called **domains**. In magnetic materials, many of the domains line up with their north poles pointing in the same direction. This makes the material

5

magnetically **dipolar** (having both a north and a south pole). The more uniform the arrangement of domains, the stronger the magnetic property of the material. **Nonmagnetic** materials do not have domains.

Magnets, like the one you used in the experiment, are made from iron, cobalt, and nickel (or alloys of these metals). The arrangement of the metal atom domains that make up the magnet creates a very strong magnetic property. The only two testing materials with magnetic properties were the iron nail and the BBs (made from steel, which contains iron), so they were the only materials to cling to the magnet.

LET'S EXPLORE

1. Are BBs and iron nails the only magnetic materials? Repeat the experiment using testing materials that are not on the materials list. Keep a record of the materials that are found to be magnetic. **Science Fair Hint:** This record can be used as part of a written report to be displayed with your project.

2. Does the magnet have to touch the testing material to attract it? Repeat the original experiment, holding the magnet very near, but not touching, the

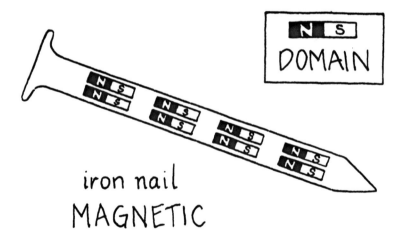

iron nail
MAGNETIC

materials. **Science Fair Hint:** Display photographs taken during the experiment that show magnets held at different distances from each testing material. Include photos of magnetic materials clinging to a magnet and record a measurement of the height the material moved to reach the magnet. Try to determine which materials have the strongest magnetic properties.

SHOW TIME!

1. Magnetic screwdrivers are useful when working with very small screws. The screw attaches itself to the magnetized tool and is prevented from being dropped. Find out more about the uses of magnets. You can display a poster with pictures representing these uses.

2. As part of an oral presentation, demonstrate how a magnet can be used to separate magnetic and nonmagnetic materials. Combine 1 teaspoon (5 ml) of salt and 1 teaspoon (5 ml) of iron filings. (You can find iron filings inside some magnetic drawing toys sold at toy stores.) Pour the mixture onto a sheet of paper. Pass a bar magnet near, but not touching, the surface of the mixture. The iron filings will cling to the magnet and the salt will stay on the paper.

CHECK IT OUT!

The ability of magnets to separate magnetic materials from nonmagnetic materials is important in many industries. Read about magnets and prepare a chart showing what you have learned. Some examples of magnets being used as separators are:

- metals separated from ore.

- archaeologists recovering sunken treasure from the ocean floor with a magnetic sweeper.

- food manufacturers preventing small iron particles that rub off of machinery from mixing with food.

- vendors sorting nonmagnetic coins from magnetic slugs and washers that are dropped into vending machines.

 **2**

More Muscle

PROBLEM

What part of a magnet has the strongest attracting ability?

Materials

scissors
ruler
string
bar magnet
masking tape
box of about 100 small paper clips
large bowl

Procedure

1. Cut two 3-foot (1-m) pieces of string.
2. Tie one end of each string to each end of the magnet.
3. Tape the free ends of the strings to the top of a door frame.
4. Adjust the length of the strings so that the magnet hangs in a level position and is at a height that is easy for you to reach.
5. Spread the paper clips in the bottom of the bowl.
6. Raise the bowl so that the magnet touches the paper clips.
7. Slowly lower the bowl.
8. Observe where the clips cling to the magnet.

Results

Most of the clinging paper clips are near the ends of the magnet.

Why?

All magnets are surrounded by an area called a **magnetic field**. This area is made of invisible lines of force coming out of the north pole of the magnet, around each side, and into the south pole of the magnet. The magnetic force lines are closest together at the poles, which

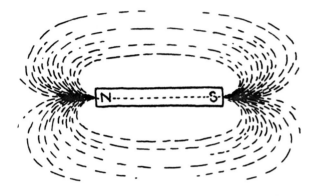

makes the poles have the strongest magnetic attraction.

LET'S EXPLORE

1. Would the shape of magnetic materials affect how they are attracted to the magnet? Repeat the experiment, replacing the paper clips with other materials such as BBs and nails. **Science Fair Hint:** Display photographs taken of the experiment to demonstrate the strongest magnetic part of each magnet.

2. Does the shape of the magnet affect its areas of strength? Repeat the original experiment using several different magnets, including round and horseshoe-shaped magnets. Raise the bowl and allow the entire magnet to touch the paper clips. **Science Fair Hint:** Secure a support beam across the top of your project display frame. Hang the magnets you used in the experiments so that you can show the magnetic material clinging to them.

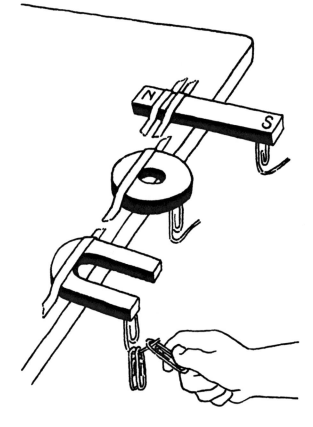

shaped magnets by taping them to a table so that part of each magnet extends over the edge. Bend open the end of a paper clip so that it forms a hook and touch it to the bottom of an extended magnet. (Do not hook it over the magnet.) Do this for each magnet. Add paper clips one at a time to each open clip until the clip pulls loose from the magnet and falls.

CHECK IT OUT!

Just as the poles of any magnetic object have a stronger magnetic pull than the rest of the object, the earth's magnetic poles have a stronger magnetic pull than the rest of the planet. Electrical particles that stream out from the sun are pulled toward the earth's magnetic poles. These electrical particles produce glowing lights in the sky called aurora borealis at the earth's North Pole and aurora australis at the earth's South Pole. Write a report on exactly how these colored lights in the sky are produced. (Information can be found on pages 104–105 of *Astronomy for Every Kid* [New York: Wiley, 1991], by Janice VanCleave.)

SHOW TIME!

Test the "muscle strength," or supporting power, of the poles of different-

 **3**

Straight Through

PROBLEM

Can magnetic forces act through paper?

Materials

sheet of paper
bar magnet
thumbtack

Procedure

1. Lay the sheet of paper on a *wooden* table.

2. Place the magnet so that its north pole is under the edge of the paper.

3. Position the tack on top of the paper where the paper covers the end of the magnet.

4. Hold the uncovered end of the magnet with your hand and move the magnet from side to side under the paper.

Results

The paper is not attracted to the magnet, but the tack is. Moving the magnet caused the tack to move.

Why?

Around every magnet is an invisible magnetic force field. Some materials, such as paper, do not stop or disrupt the pattern of the force field. Materials that allow a magnetic force field to pass through without any disruptions in the magnetic field are said to be **nonperme-**

able. Materials that seem to absorb the magnetic lines of force are said to be **permeable**. Nonpermeable materials *are not* attracted to a magnet, whereas permeable materials *are* attracted to a magnet. The magnetic field passes through the paper with no change in the direction of the field; thus, the paper is nonpermeable and nonmagnetic. The magnetic field moves in and around the tack; thus, the tack is said to be permeable to the magnetic field.

LET'S EXPLORE

1. Do both ends of the magnet behave the same way? Repeat the experiment,

turning the magnet around so that its south pole is under the edge of the paper.

2. Would thicker paper allow the magnetic field to pass through? Repeat the experiment twice, replacing the sheet of paper with thicker paper and with cardboard. **Science Fair Hint:** Photographs taken during each testing and diagrams with labels describing the procedure can be used as part of a project display along with paper samples.

3. Do materials other than paper allow magnetic force lines to pass through?

Repeat the original experiment, replacing the paper with different materials, such as wax paper, aluminum foil, plastic wrap, a cookie sheet, a metal cake-server, or a glass bowl. **Science Fair Hint:** Record and use your results as part of a project display along with the samples tested.

SHOW TIME!

1. To compare the strength of two different-sized magnets, place one magnet under a few pages of a book. Place a paper clip on top of the pages, so that the paper clip is attracted by

the magnet. Start putting more and more pages between the magnet and the paper clip until the paper clip is no longer attracted to the magnet. Now replace the first magnet with the second magnet, and repeat the procedure to compare the number of pages through which each magnet is

able to attract the paper clip. The results of this experiment can be displayed along with diagrams and/or photographs.

2. To test the nonpermeability of liquids, pour a clear liquid such as water or corn syrup into a glass. Place a magnet inside a plastic bag and tie a string around the top of the bag. Stir iron filings into the liquid and quickly lower the plastic bag into the liquid. Make and display drawings of the procedure and results.

CHECK IT OUT!

What is in the magnetic force field that passes through nonpermeable material but is absorbed by permeable material? Some scientists think that invisible particles called **magnetic monopoles** fly out of the north pole of a magnet, loop around the magnet, and then fly back into the south pole of the magnet. Your parent, teacher, or librarian can assist you in finding information about magnetic force fields and about nonpermeable and permeable materials. When presenting these materials, use a poster showing examples of the two types of materials.

 **4**

Get Away

PROBLEM

What happens when the north pole of a magnet is placed near the north or south pole of another magnet?

Materials

scissors
ruler
sheet of paper
paper hole-punch
string
2 bar magnets
masking tape

Procedure

1. Make a paper sling to hold the first magnet by cutting a 1-inch × 8-inch (2.5-cm × 20-cm) strip from the paper.

2. Use the hole-punch to make a hole in each end of the paper strip.

3. Bend the strip of paper to bring the holes at each end together. Then put a 12-inch (30-cm) string through the holes, and knot the string at one end to tie the holes together.

4. Place the first magnet in the sling.

5. Tape the free end of the string to the edge of a *wooden* table so that the magnet hangs horizontally.

6. Hold the second magnet in your hand so that its north pole is near, but not touching, the south pole of the hanging magnet.

7. Observe the motion of the hanging magnet.

8. Steady the sling, then hold the south pole of the magnet in your hand near the south pole of the hanging magnet.

9. Again, observe the motion of the hanging magnet.

10. Repeat, holding the north pole of the second magnet in your hand near the north pole of the hanging magnet.

11. Observe the motion of the hanging magnet.

Results

The hanging magnet moves toward the hand-held magnet when the poles are different (north near south). When like poles (north near north, or south near south) are held close to each other, the hanging magnet moves away from the hand-held magnet.

Why?

The poles of magnets exert attractive and repulsive forces upon each other. "Unlike" (north and south) magnetic poles attract each other, and "like" (north and north, or south and south) magnetic poles repel each other. The magnetic force field coming out of the north pole actually moves toward and enters the south pole of the second magnet, thus drawing the two magnets toward each other. When two north poles or two south poles are brought together, the magnetic force fields of like poles push against each other, causing the magnets to move apart.

LET'S EXPLORE

1. Is it necessary to have one of the magnets suspended? Remove the magnet from the sling and place it on a smooth table. Repeat the experiment, recording any movement of the magnet on the table when the hand-held magnet moves toward it.

2. Does the attraction and repulsion of magnetic poles hold true for all shapes of magnets? Repeat the original experi-

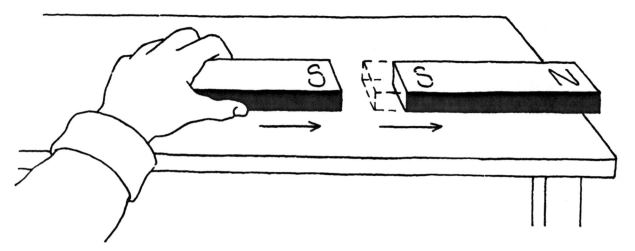

ment using different shapes of magnets. Try mixing and matching the shapes of the magnets, such as suspending a bar-shaped magnet while holding a round magnet. **Science Fair Hint:** Photographs taken during the experiments, as well as diagrams showing the position of the magnets when like and unlike poles repel or attract each other, can be used as part of a project display. Label the poles of the magnets on the diagrams, and use arrows to indicate the direction that each magnet moved.

SHOW TIME!

Tape the ends of a thread about 12 inches (30 cm) long to opposite sides of a small piece of magnetic craft tape (found at arts and crafts stores). Tape the loop formed by the thread to a table so that the magnet hangs over the edge. Hang a second magnet level with, and as close as possible to, the first magnet without touching them to each other. Spin one of the magnets a few times to wind the thread, and then release. Use the knowledge that the outside surface of each side

of the tape is polar to explain the motion of the two magnets. Hang these magnets as part of a project display, along with diagrams explaining their action.

CHECK IT OUT!

A magnetic levitation train (called a "Maglev") floats above the track because of the repulsion between a magnet on the train and the magnetized track. Write a report about the use of magnets in this modern transportation system. Is it considered safe? Is it faster than traditional trains? Would it be more ecologically sound?

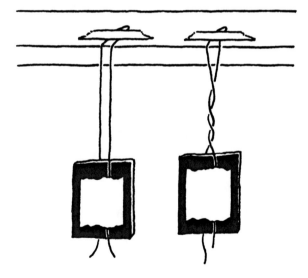

19

 **5**

Pointer

PROBLEM

How does a compass work?

Materials

compass

Procedure

NOTE: Never touch a compass with a magnet. Touching a compass with a strong magnet can change the polarity of the compass needle, causing the end marked north to become a south pole and all directions to be reversed.

1. Place the compass on a *wooden* table away from magnets or magnetic materials.

2. Observe the compass needle and determine which end is the north pole. The north end of the needle will have some distinguishing mark, such as an arrowhead or a color.

3. Printed on the compass are the letters N, E, S, and W, which represent the directions north, east, south, and west. Turn the compass on the table until the letter N is even with the north pole of the compass needle.

Results

The compass needle points north. The printed letters on the compass indicate the directions east, south, and west.

Why?

A **compass** is an instrument used to determine directions by means of a magnetic needle that always points to the earth's magnetic north pole. The main part of a compass is its magnetized needle. This needle is balanced so that when the compass is held horizontally, the needle can swing around freely. The magnetized needle acts like any bar magnet with both a north and a south pole. The needle swings into a north-to-south position as the poles of the magnetic needle line up with the magnetic lines of force around the earth. All the compass directions are easily determined when the compass is positioned with the north pole of the needle pointing to the N printed on the compass.

LET'S EXPLORE

1. Would the compass work if you held it in your hand? Repeat the experiment, holding the compass in a horizontal position.

2. Does it matter where you stand while holding the compass? Repeat the original experiment in different rooms, as well as at different places outside. **Science Fair Hint**: Diagrams with instructions for how to work a compass can be used as part of a project display.

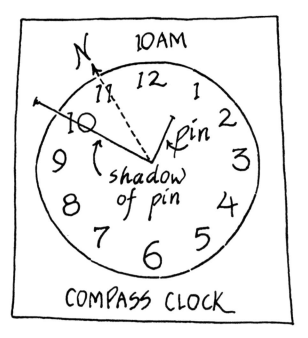

COMPASS CLOCK

3. What effect would a magnet or a magnetic material have on the compass? Repeat the original experiment by placing a magnet or a magnetic material, such as a paper clip, near but not touching the compass.

SHOW TIME!

Make and display different kinds of compasses.

- A nonmagnetic *compass clock* can be constructed by drawing the face of a clock on a paper circle. Place the paper on an outside surface in direct sunlight. Stick a pin in the middle of the circle and turn the paper until the shadow of the pin falls on the correct time. *NOTE: Do not use daylight savings time, because during daylight savings time your solar clock will read one hour earlier than your watch.* North will always be halfway between the shadow and the number 12 on the paper clock.

- You can also make a *floating compass*. Cut a paper ring to fit around the outside of a bowl. Mark the four compass directions N, E, S, and W on the paper ring. Fill the bowl with water. Cut a 1-inch × 1-inch (2.5-cm × 2.5-cm) piece from a sponge. Place the sponge piece in the water and lay a magnetized needle on top of it. (To temporarily magnetize the needle, lay it on a bar magnet for two minutes with the eye of the needle at the north end of the magnet.) The needle and the sponge will swing around so that the point of the needle faces north. Rotate the paper collar around the bowl so that the point of the needle points to the N on the paper.

bowl of water

needle

FLOATING COMPASS

CHECK IT OUT!

In the 12th and 13th centuries, Arabian and Chinese astronomers discovered that magnetic stones suspended from strings always turned toward the same direction. In the 14th century, European navigators began to explore the oceans with reasonable assurance that they could find their way back home with the aid of a magnetic compass. Find out more about compasses. Discuss information such as:

- what makes a mariner's or a ship's compass special.

- types of magnets used in the past and in the present.

- uses of compasses in our modern technological world.

- how a gyrocompass works.

 **6**

Tug-of-War

PROBLEM

How can the strength of two magnets be compared?

Materials

compass
2 plastic rulers
2 bar magnets

Procedure

NOTE: Never touch a compass with a magnet. Touching a compass with a strong magnet can change the polarity of the compass needle, causing the end marked north to become a south pole and all directions to be reversed.

1. Place the compass on a *wooden* table. Be sure that no magnets or magnetic materials are nearby.

2. Turn the compass so that the north pole of the needle points to the N printed on the case.

3. Lay the first ruler on the west side of the compass, so that it points away from the compass (see diagram).

4. Place the second ruler on the east side of the compass.

5. Lay the first magnet on the west side of the compass at the 6-inch (15-cm) mark of the first ruler. Place the south end of the magnet toward the compass.

6. Place the second magnet on the east side of the compass at the 6-inch (15-cm) mark of the second ruler. Again, place the south end of the magnet toward the compass.

7. Observe the position of the compass needle.

6 inches (15 cm)

6 inches (15 cm)

Results

There are three possible positions for the needle, depending upon the strength of the magnets: it will continue to point toward the north, N; it will move toward the east, E; or it will move toward the west, W.

Why?

A compass has a free-moving, magnetized, needle-shaped magnet. The needle swings into a north-to-south position as its poles line up with the magnetic lines of force around the earth. Placing magnets near the compass causes the needle to move from its natural north-to-south position. The south pole of the magnet attracts the north pole of the compass's magnetized needle, causing it to swing toward the magnet. The two magnets placed on opposite sides of the compass pull on the compass needle, as in a game of tug-of-war. If the magnets are of equal strength and at an equal distance from the compass, their pull on the needle is balanced and the needle continues to point toward the magnetic north pole of the earth. If one of the magnets is stronger than the other, that magnet wins the magnetic tug-of-war and the compass needle swings toward the stronger magnet.

LET'S EXPLORE

1. Would placing the north ends of the magnets toward the compass affect the results? Repeat the experiment, this time placing the north pole of each magnet toward the compass.

2. Do the magnets have to be placed east and west of the compass? Try placing them to the north and south instead, and repeat the original experiment.

SHOW TIME!

To compare the strengths of two magnets, place the compass and the rulers in the same position as in the original tug-of-

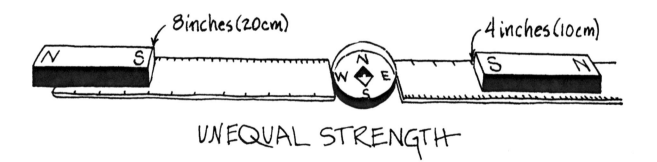

UNEQUAL STRENGTH

war experiment. Place the first magnet on the west-side ruler, with its south pole facing the west side of the compass. Slowly move the magnet across the ruler toward the compass; stop the magnet when the compass needle points north-west, NW. Lay the second magnet on the east-side ruler, with its south pole facing the compass. Slowly move the magnet toward the compass until the compass needle points north, N. The magnet farther from the compass is the stronger magnet. Display diagrams showing the position of magnets of *equal* strength and magnets of *unequal* strength.

CHECK IT OUT!

A magnetometer is an instrument that measures the strength of magnets by moving the magnets until their magnet forces balance. Magnetometers are used to measure the intensity of the earth's magnetic field at a given spot. Read about these instruments and write a report that includes information such as how magnetometers:

- detect valuable ore deposits.

- are used to search for oil.

- are used by geologists to determine rock structure beneath land masses and the ocean.

7

Swinger

PROBLEM

Can magnetic attraction overcome the pull of gravity?

Materials

2 bar magnets
sewing needle

Procedure

1. Place the first magnet on a *wooden* table.

2. Hold the second magnet about 2 inches (5 cm) above the magnet laying on the table. Position the two magnets so that opposite poles (north and south) are facing each other.

3. Touch the point of the sewing needle to the bottom of the top magnet.

4. Lower the top magnet so that the hanging needle is very close to, but not touching, the magnet laying on the table.

5. Use your finger to push the bottom of the needle to one side, and release the needle as if swinging a pendulum.

6. Observe the movement of the needle.

Results

The needle swings quickly back and forth for a few seconds, and then stops in a straight-up-and-down position between the two magnets.

Why?

Touching the needle to the magnet magnetizes the needle. The needle becomes an extended part of the magnet's pole that it is touching. Because "unlike" magnetic poles (north and south) are attracted to each other, the eye end of the needle is attracted to the opposite pole of the lower magnet. **Gravity** plus the downward magnetic pull toward the lower magnet do not produce a force strong enough to move the needle away from the magnet it touches. From point A in the diagram, the needle moves toward point B because of both the downward pull of gravity and the attraction toward the lower magnet. The needle passes point B and swings upward to point C, where it is again pulled down by gravity and the attractive magnet pull toward the lower magnet. The height of the swing decreases with each swing, until finally the needle stops and stands still in a vertical position. The strong magnetic pull of the magnet touching the needle keeps the needle from falling, but the lower magnet's pull keeps the needle from swinging freely.

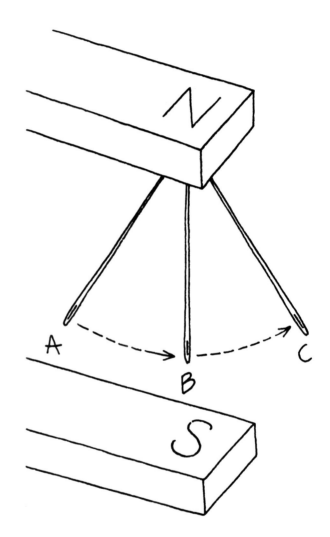

LET'S EXPLORE

1. Would standing the needle on the lower magnet affect its swing? Repeat the experiment, placing the point of the needle on the lower magnet. Observe any changes in the speed and time that the needle continues to swing.

2. Would a different-sized needle affect the results? Repeat the original experiment twice, first using a smaller needle, and then using a larger needle. Observe and record any differences in the speed and time that each needle swings.

SHOW TIME!

1. Use the magnets and needle as part of a project display. So that you do not have to hold the magnet, support the upper magnet on a stack of books. As part of an oral presentation, demonstrate the movement of the needle when suspended on the top and bottom magnet. Display diagrams showing the forces acting on the needle during its swing.

2. How does the shape of magnets affect their purpose? Examine different kinds of magnets and their uses. Collect and display different-shaped magnets and/or pictures of magnets, such as magnetic bulletin boards, refrigerator magnets, and magnetized screwdrivers.

CHECK IT OUT!

Read about the magnetic fields around magnets of different shapes and discover why a horseshoe magnet can hold up more magnetic material than can a bar magnet of the same magnetic strength. Diagrams showing the magnetic field around each shaped magnet can be part of a report. Enlarged copies of the diagrams can be displayed as part of a project.

 **8**

Which Way?

PROBLEM?

How can you identify the poles of an unmarked magnet?

Materials

masking tape
3 sheets of paper
compass
marking pen
scissors
ruler
paper hole-punch
string
bar magnet

Procedure

NOTE: Never touch a compass with a magnet. Touching a compass with a strong magnet can change the polarity of the compass needle, causing the end marked north to become a south pole and all directions to be reversed.

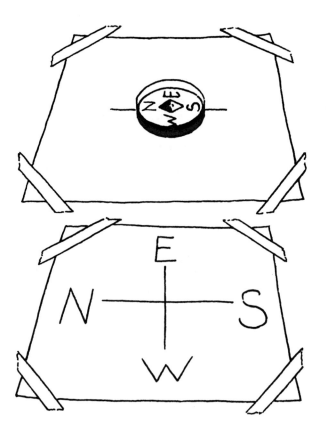

1. Make a paper compass by taping one sheet of paper to the top of a *wooden* table. Be sure that there are no magnetic materials on or near the table.

2. Place the real compass in the center of the paper.

3. Use the marking pen to draw marks on the paper at the four main compass points (N, E, S, and W).

4. Remove the real compass. With your pen, connect the paper compass points with straight lines and label the directions as shown in the diagram on page 32.

5. Make a paper sling to hold the magnet by cutting a 1-inch × 8-inch (2.5-cm × 20-cm) strip from a second sheet of paper.

6. Use the hole-punch to make a hole in each end of the paper strip.

7. Bend the strip of paper to bring the holes at each end together. Then put a 12-inch (30-cm) string through the holes, and knot the string at one end to tie the holes together.

8. Wrap a piece of paper around the magnet and secure it with tape, in order to cover up any identifying pole-markings.

9. Place the magnet in the paper sling so that the magnet hangs horizontally.

10. Hold the end of the string and hang the magnet over the paper compass taped to the table, until the magnet's ends point steadily in a north-to-south direction.

11. Use masking tape and the marking pen to label a large N and S at the ends of the magnet that are pointing north and south.

Results

It takes about one minute for the swinging magnet to come to rest in line with the north-to-south line on the paper compass.

Why?

A magnetic force field surrounds the earth. Any suspended magnet will align itself with this magnetic field. The north end of the hanging magnet always points to the earth's magnetic north pole, and the south end of the magnet points to the earth's magnetic south pole. Identifying the north and south pole of a magnet is called finding the **polarity** of the magnet.

LET'S EXPLORE

1. Do all magnets, regardless of their shape, align with the earth's magnetic field and point in a north-to-south direction? Repeat the experiment using different-shaped magnets. **Science Fair Hint:** Display diagrams and photographs of hanging magnets of different shapes and sizes.

2. Does the size of the magnet affect the way it behaves? Repeat the experiment using different sizes of bar, round, and horseshoe magnets.

3. Would changing the size of the paper sling change the behavior of the magnet? Repeat the original experiment twice, first using a wider paper strip, and then using a narrower strip.

SHOW TIME!

1. Plastic magnetic strips found in craft stores have north and south poles on opposite sides of the strip. A 2-inch (5-cm) magnetic strip can be tested to find its polarity. Attach a piece of string to the magnetic piece, and then hang the string so that it is allowed to turn freely. Use a compass to determine the direction of the earth's magnetic north pole. Mark the north and south sides of the strip.

2. Magnetize a needle by allowing it to lie on a magnet for two minutes. Tie a thread to the center of the magnetized needle and suspend it inside a glass jar. Use a compass to determine which end of the needle points toward the north. Once you have identified the polarity of the needle, it can be used as a compass. Display the hanging compass as part of a project.

CHECK IT OUT!

At first, the stones that attracted small pieces of iron were called *Magnete stones* in honor of a Greek tribe, the Magnetes. Later, the stones were called *magnetite* and then, when it was discovered that

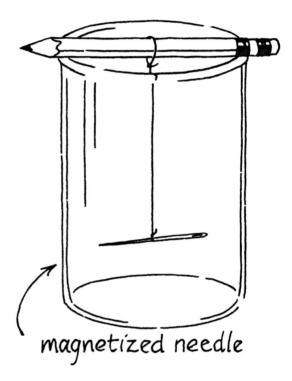

HOMEMADE COMPASS

magnetized needle

these suspended stones always point north, the name changed to *lodestone*. Write a report about the first magnets. Include the meaning of the word "lodestone," as well as information about the first crude compasses made from this north-seeking stone.

 **9**

Line Up

PROBLEM

How can you "see" a magnetic field?

Materials

2 bar magnets
2 sheets of paper
large paper cup
iron filings (found in magnetic drawing
    toys sold at toy stores)

Procedure

1. Arrange the 2 magnets end to end on a
wooden table, with their north poles
about 2 inches (5 cm) apart.

2. Cover the magnets with the first sheet
of paper.

3. Fill the paper cup with the iron filings.
Slowly sprinkle some of the filings
over the part of the paper that is covering the magnets.

4. Observe the pattern formed by the
iron filings on the paper.

5. After removing the first sheet of paper,
rearrange the magnets so that the
north pole of the first magnet is about
2 inches (5 cm) away from the south
pole of the second magnet.

6. Cover the magnets with the second
sheet of paper. Sprinkle the remaining
iron filings over the part of the paper
that is covering the magnets.

7. Observe the pattern formed by the
iron filings on the paper.

iron filings

Results

The iron filings form curved lines around each magnet, regardless of how the magnets are arranged. The pattern of the filings changes near the magnet poles (ends) that have been placed near another magnet. The lines formed by the filings bend away from each other at the ends where the north poles face each other. When north and south poles face each other, lines of iron filings curve from the end of the first magnet toward the end of the second magnet.

Why?

Every magnet has an invisible magnetic field around it. This field is made up of lines of force that attract magnetic material such as iron filings. The filings form a pattern as they line up in the direction of the magnetic lines of force. The lines of force around each magnet come out of the north pole, loop around the magnet, and enter the magnet's south pole. The magnetic forces of two "like" poles, such as two north poles, repel each other. Placing two north poles near each other results in the iron filings at the facing ends being pushed away from the neighboring magnet. "Unlike" poles of magnets attract each other. Placing north and south poles of magnets near each other results in a magnetic field that comes out of the north end of the first magnet and moves toward the facing south pole of the second magnet. The iron filings line up with their force field forming a bridge of filings between the two magnets.

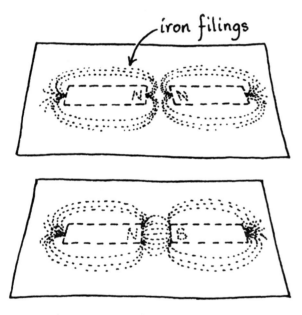

MAGNETIC FIELDS

LET'S EXPLORE

1. Would placing the south poles of the magnets near each other produce a different pattern? Repeat the experiment, placing the magnets so that their south poles face each other.

2. Would laying the magnets side by side change the pattern of the iron filings?

Repeat the original experiment, placing the magnets so that they are lined up side by side.

3. Does the shape of the magnet affect the pattern of the iron filings? Repeat the original experiment using different-shaped magnets. **Science Fair Hint:** Photographs and drawings showing the iron filing patterns around the magnets can be used as part of a project display.

SHOW TIME!

On a piece of cardboard, position different-shaped magnets. In one area, position the magnets with "like" poles facing each other, and in a second area, have the "unlike" poles of the magnets facing each other. Cover the magnets with a large sheet of white paper. Sprinkle iron filings over the surface of the paper. Gently tap the paper with your finger and the filings will form a pattern of the force field around the magnets. Use a spray bottle to cover the paper with a fine mist of white vinegar. Allow the paper to remain undisturbed for several hours—enough time for the iron filings to rust. Later, turn the paper over and brush off the rusty filings.

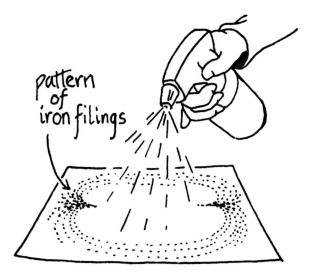

pattern of iron filings

The rust marks will remain on the paper to record the shapes of the magnetic fields around each magnet.

CHECK IT OUT!

Read about Michael Faraday. This 19th-century English scientist was the first person to make it possible to visualize magnetic lines of force around a magnet. Find out how this self-taught genius with no math or science training became someone whose advice was sought by important scientists of his day. Include this information in your project.

 **10**

Plotting

PROBLEM

What is the direction of the magnetic lines of force around a magnet?

Materials

bar magnet
sheet of paper
compass
pencil

Procedure

NOTE: Never touch a compass with a magnet. Touching a compass with a strong magnet can change the polarity of the compass needle, causing the end marked north to become a south pole and all directions to be reversed.

1. Place the magnet near the bottom edge of the sheet of paper.

2. Place the compass on the paper, about 1 inch (2.5 cm) above the north-pole side of the magnet.

3. Use the pencil to mark a dot on the paper in front of the north pole of the compass pointer.

4. Move the compass forward until the south pole of the compass needle points to the dot.

5. Mark a new dot on the paper in front of the north pole of the compass pointer.

6. Again, move the compass forward until the south pole of its pointer is in front of the second dot.

7. Continue making dots on the paper in front of the compass's north-pole pointer until the compass reaches the south-pole end of the magnet.

8. Repeat the procedure, this time starting at the south-pole side of the magnet.

9. Observe the pattern of the plotted dots.

Results

The plotted dots form a curved pattern from one end of the magnet to the other.

Why?

The invisible magnetic field around the magnet is made up of lines of force that move out of the north pole of the magnet and into the south pole. Since "unlike" poles attract each other, the north pole of the compass needle always turns toward the south pole of the magnet. Each time the compass is moved, the compass pointer lines up with the line of force.

LET'S EXPLORE

1. Are there lines of force at the ends of the magnet? Repeat the experiment, this time placing the compass at the corner of the north pole of the magnet.

2. Does the pattern change with different-shaped magnets? Repeat the original experiment using round-shaped and horseshoe-shaped magnets.

3. Do the lines of force cross each other? Repeat the original experiment, placing the compass next to the previous line. Mark the dots as before, and observe the position of the second force-field line. Different lines of force can be plotted by starting the compass in a new position, but you will discover that force lines do not cross each other. **Science Fair Hint**: Take photographs as you mark each dot in front of the compass pointer. Display the photographs and the plotted dots showing the pattern of the force fields around the side and end of the magnet.

SHOW TIME!

Is the force field three-dimensional? Magnetize two needles by laying them on a strong magnet for two minutes. Hold the eye end of one needle. Suspend the second needle by touching the points of the two needles together. Slowly move the needles from one end of the magnet to the other. Observe the movement of the hanging needle.

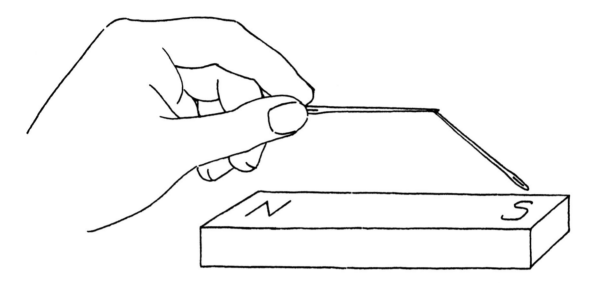

CHECK IT OUT!

The earth behaves as if it contains a large magnet that produces magnetic lines of force around the globe. As the earth revolves around the sun, there are fluctuations in the earth's magnetic field. Think about these questions:

- Why do the major changes in the earth's magnetic field occur during the **equinox** (when the sun is in line with the earth's equator), while minimum changes occur during the **solstice** (when the sun is farthest either north or south of the earth's equator)?

- During what months of the year do these major and minor changes take place?

 **11**

Protector

PROBLEM

How can magnetic materials be shielded from a magnetic force field?

Materials

scissors
ruler
cardboard
2 pencils
masking tape
bar magnet
10 paper clips
stainless steel cake-server

Procedure

1. Cut two 8-inch × 4-inch (20-cm × 10-cm) cardboard pieces.

2. Put the pencils between the cardboard pieces, as shown in the diagram.

3. Tape the ends of the cardboard pieces together to secure the cardboard-and-air sandwich.

4. Tape the magnet near the edge of the top piece of cardboard.

5. Place all 10 paper clips on a *wooden* table.

6. Hold the cardboard sandwich high above the paper clips.

7. Slowly lower the cardboard sandwich until it is just above, but not touching, the clips.

8. Observe any movement of the paper clips.

9. Without moving the cardboard, slowly insert the cake-server between the two pieces of cardboard.

10. Again, observe any movement of the paper clips.

45

Results

The paper clips are first pulled up and cling to the bottom of the cardboard-and-air sandwich. The clips fall when the metal cake-server is inserted between the cardboard pieces.

Why?

The magnetic lines of force from the magnet pass through the cardboard and air, as indicated by the attraction of the paper clips toward the magnet. Materials that allow magnetic lines of force to pass through them are said to be **nonpermeable**. The stainless steel cake-server acts as a magnetic shield. The force lines coming from the north pole of the magnet do not pass through the cake-server and then continue to move outward. Instead, they are gathered in, travel down the metal server, and re-enter the magnet at its south pole. Materials that gather magnetic lines of force are said to be **permeable**. Only magnetic materials are permeable.

LET'S EXPLORE

1. What other materials are **permeable**? Repeat the experiment, but replace the cake-server with other materials such as paper, glass, wood, plastic, rubber, and aluminum foil. **Science Fair Hint:** Use magazine pictures to make a poster of permeable and nonpermeable items. The poster can be used as part of a project display.

2. Does the shape of the magnet affect the permeability of materials held near the magnet? Repeat the original experiment using different-shaped magnets. **Science Fair Hint:** Display drawings or photographs to indicate the results of using different-shaped magnets.

SHOW TIME!

Use iron filings to show the effect of permeable and nonpermeable materials on magnetic lines of force. Place a horseshoe magnet on a table, with an iron nail near but not touching the poles of the magnet. Cover the magnet with a sheet of paper. Sprinkle iron filings on the part of the paper that is covering the magnet. Repeat the experiment, but replace the nail with a wooden stick. Make drawings and/or take photographs of the patterns formed by the iron filings. These diagrams and photographs can be displayed

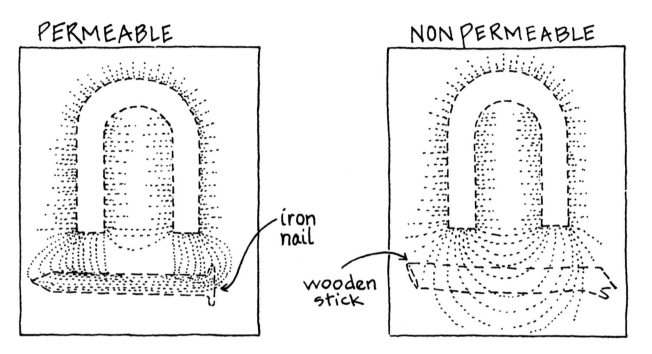

PERMEABLE

NON PERMEABLE

iron
nail

wooden
stick

to show the effect of permeable materials and nonpermeable materials.

CHECK IT OUT!

Like a bar magnet, the earth has a magnetic field around it. This field, called the **magnetosphere**, protects the earth from powerful space radiation. Read about this protective shield. You could include this information in an oral report and create a diagram showing the shape of the magnetosphere with its tail-like extension trailing outward toward the sun.

47

 **12**

Dipper

PROBLEM

How can you follow the direction of magnetic lines of force around a magnet?

Materials

bar magnet
scissors
ruler
sewing thread
sewing needle

Procedure

1. Lay the magnet on a *wooden* table.

2. Cut a 1-foot (30-cm) piece of thread, and tie the thread piece to the center of the needle. (Don't put the thread through the eye of the needle.)

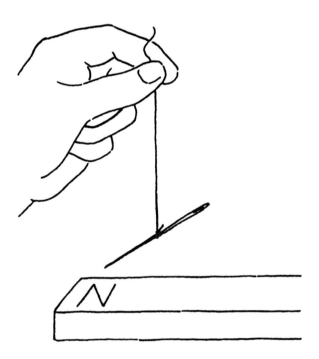

3. Hold the free end of the thread with one hand. Move the needle back and forth through the knot in the thread until it hangs in a horizontal position (parallel, or level, with the tabletop). *NOTE: A needle mounted on a horizontal axis and allowed to swing in a vertical plane is known as a **dipping needle.***

4. Move your arm so that the needle is about 2 inches (5 cm) above the magnet.

5. Slowly move the hanging needle across the magnet, from one end of the magnet to the other.

6. Observe the position of the needle as it travels above the magnet.

Results

The needle is vertical (straight up and down) when it hangs above the ends of the magnet; it is horizontal when it is above the center of the magnet, and at various positions between horizontal and vertical as it is moved from the end toward the center of the magnet.

Why?

The invisible magnetic field around every magnet is made up of lines of force that move out of its north pole and into its south pole. The hanging needle follows these lines of force. Its freedom to move up and down allows it to dip toward the magnet at different places. This change in the needle's position is called **inclination**. (Any change from a horizontal position is an inclination.) At the poles, where the force lines are closest together, the inclination or dipping of the needle is so great that the needle hangs in a vertical position. The change in the amount of inclination of the needle as it moves from one end of the magnet to the other indicates that the invisible magnetic force lines near the center of the magnet spread apart and weaken.

LET'S EXPLORE

1. Does the distance of the needle from the magnet affect the inclination of the needle? Repeat the experiment, holding the needle at different heights from the surface of the magnet. **Science Fair Hint**: Display photographs taken during the experiment to demonstrate

the inclination of a dipping needle due to the magnetic field around a magnet.

2. Would the size of the needle affect its inclination? Repeat the original experiment using different sizes of needles. Nails may be used instead of, or in addition to, needles. **Science Fair Hint**: As part of an oral presentation, demonstrate the use of a dipping needle. Use several sizes of needles (or nails), and hold each at different heights above the magnet to demonstrate the affect of size and distance from the magnet.

SHOW TIME!

Place a bar magnet under a sheet of paper. On top of the paper, draw a diagram of the earth with a diameter the length of a bar magnet. Use a stack of books to suspend a ruler above the drawing. Hang three dipping needles from the ruler, two above the poles and one above the center of the magnet, to indicate the inclination at the earth's magnetic equator and polar areas.

CHECK IT OUT!

Sir William Gilbert, a 17th-century physician and physicist, observed that a magnetic needle free to move up and down dips toward the earth at many places. Read about how he laid the foundation for our present-day knowledge of the earth's magnetism.

 **13**

Back and Forth

PROBLEM

How can you measure the earth's magnetism at different locations?

Materials

sheet of paper
masking tape
small iron nail
bar magnet
scissors
ruler
thread
compass
pencil
timer

Procedure

1. Roll the paper and tape it to form a large open-ended cylinder. Place the cylinder on the floor next to a *wooden* table.

2. Magnetize the nail by laying it on the magnet for three minutes.

3. Cut a 36-inch (1-m) piece of thread, and tie one end to the center of the magnetized nail.

4. Tape the free end of the thread to the edge of the table so that the nail hangs inside and about 2 inches (5 cm) below the top of the cylinder. The cylinder will block any breeze that might move the nail.

5. Set the compass on the floor near the cylinder.

6. Use the pencil to turn the nail in an east-to-west direction, as indicated by the compass.

7. Ask a helper to start the timer when the nail is released. Have your helper announce the end of one minute.

8. Count the number of **oscillations** (one back-and-forth movement) the nail makes during one minute.

9. Repeat the experiment twice more.

10. Average the results of the three trials by adding the number of oscillations together and dividing the sum by three.

Example:

Trial #1	17 oscillations
Trial #2	16 oscillations
Trial #3	18 oscillations
Total	51 oscillations

Average: 51 ÷ 3 = 17 oscillations

Results

The number of oscillations the nail makes will depend on the part of the earth where you live.

Why?

One back-and-forth motion is called an **oscillation**. The number of oscillations made by the hanging nail varies with the distance you are from the magnetic north or south pole. The slowest oscillation would be at the **magnetic equator** (the imaginary line between the north and south magnetic poles that divides the earth in half). The oscillations increase as you approach either the north or south magnetic pole. The magnetic lines of force are closer at the poles and thus have a stronger pull on the magnetized nail, causing it to swing faster.

LET'S EXPLORE

1. Would a different-sized nail affect the number of oscillations? Repeat the experiment twice, first using a smaller nail, and then using a larger nail.

2. Does the size of the thread affect the oscillation of the nail? Repeat the original experiment using a thicker string to suspend the nail.

3. Is there a difference in the strength of the earth's magnetic field in your neighborhood? Repeat the original experiment at different locations, such as at school or at the homes of friends. If you have the opportunity to travel, take the materials with you and measure the earth's magnetism in a different town. **Science Fair Hint:** Make a map of the area where you performed

the experiment, with the results of the experiment printed on it. A summary stating the results should be printed at the bottom of the map.

SHOW TIME!

Simulate the testing of the earth's magnetic field closer to its magnetic poles by placing a magnet near the hanging nail. Count the oscillations of the nail with the magnet at different distances from the nail. Use this experiment as part of your display. Attach the string to a support placed across the top of your project display, with the nail hanging freely in the center of the project. Use a magnet to demonstrate the change in the speed of the oscillations as the strength of the magnetic field increases.

CHECK IT OUT!

Conduct special research of the measurement of the earth's magnetic field. With the assistance of your parents and teacher, you can correspond with students in different geographic locations. In previous experiments, you determined if the size of the nail and string affected the results. Use the results of these experiments to instruct your "around-the-world laboratory helpers" about the type of materials needed for their testings. The results can be displayed as a science fair project.

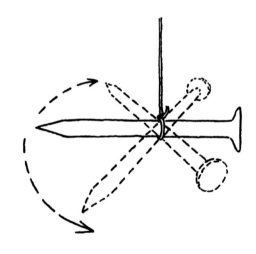

 **14**

Mapping

PROBLEM

How can you determine the direction of the earth's magnetic field at different times in the past?

Materials

teaspoon (5-ml)
plaster of paris
water
paper cup
paper towel
iron filings (found in magnetic drawing
  toys sold at toy stores)
bar magnet
sheet of paper
compass
marking pen

Procedure

1. Mix 4 teaspoons (20 ml) of plaster of paris with 2 teaspoons (10 ml) of water in the paper cup. Wipe the spoon clean with the paper towel. *WARNING: Do not wash the plaster down the drain, as it might harden and clog the drain.*

plaster
with
iron filings

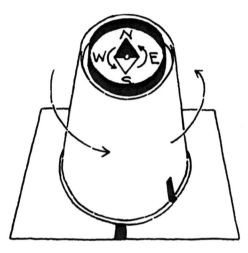

2. Pour ½ teaspoon (2.5 ml) of iron filings into the plaster mixture. Stir well.

3. Set the paper cup on top of the north-pole end of the magnet.

4. Allow the plaster to harden (about 15 to 20 minutes). Then remove the magnet.

5. Place the sheet of paper on a *wooden* table.

6. Turn the cup upside down on top of the paper. Keep the magnet and any magnetic materials away from the cup.

7. Place the compass on the cup's upturned bottom.

8. Place the tip of the marking pen against the cup, about 1 inch (2.5 cm) above the paper, and draw a thick line on the cup down to the paper. Continue the same thick line on the paper for about 1 inch (2.5 cm) away from the cup.

9. Make sure the thick lines are aligned before moving the cup.

10. Rotate the cup one quarter of a turn and stop.

11. Wait until the compass needle stops moving, and then note the direction that the compass needle is pointing.

12. Continue to turn the cup, one quarter of a turn at a time, and note the direction of the compass needle. Do this until a complete rotation has been made.

Results

The needle on the compass points in a different direction after each quarter-turn of the cup.

Why?

The needle of a compass is a magnet that lines up with the earth's magnetic lines of force. The ends of the needle point toward the magnetic north and south poles of the earth. The iron filings in the plaster become magnetized when placed near a magnet, and line up with the magnetic lines of force around the magnet. When the plaster of paris hardens, the tiny iron particles are held in place. The hardened plaster, with the iron particles frozen in place, acts like a magnet with magnetic north and south poles. Rotating the cup changes the direction that the iron particles point. As a result, the compass needle continues to line up with the magnetic field that surrounds the iron particles, instead of with the magnetic force field of the earth. The earth's magnetic force field is presently pointing in a different direction than in past times. Evidence for this shift is found in magnetic rocks. It is believed that grains of magnetic material in rocks formed from hot lava, or that melted rocks lined up with the earth's magnetic force field. When the liquid cooled and became a solid, the magnetic grains were frozen into place and formed a map pointing in the direction of the earth's magnetic poles. These magnetic maps indicate that the magnetic poles of the earth have moved to different places over time.

LET'S EXPLORE

1. Would it affect the results if the cup were placed on the south pole of the magnet? Repeat the experiment, placing the cup over the south pole of the magnet.

2. Would larger particles of magnetic materials line up with the magnetic field of the magnet and produce the same results as the tiny particles of iron filings? Repeat the original experiment, but substitute steel BBs for the iron filings. **Science Fair Hint:** Display the cups of plaster containing iron filings and BBs, along with a compass that can be used to demonstrate any change in polarity as the cups are rotated.

SHOW TIME!

You can make a model of the earth that shows the position of the magnetic and geographic poles by pushing a plastic or aluminum knitting needle completely

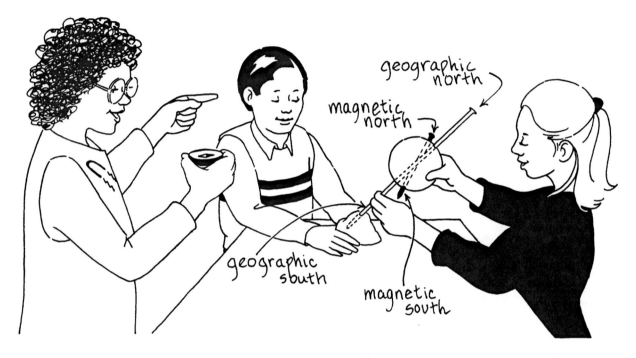

through a Styrofoam™ ball, as in the diagram. Magnetize a long nail so that the head becomes the north pole. Insert the nail completely through the ball at a slight angle to the knitting needle. Tilt the sphere and push the needle into a lump of modeling clay so that the head of the needle points up at an angle. Label the magnetic and geographic poles on the sphere. A compass can be used to demonstrate that the nail attracts the compass needle but the knitting needle does not.

CHECK IT OUT!

Where are the earth's magnetic north and south poles? Read about the magnetic poles and draw a map showing the present location of the earth's geographic and magnetic poles. It is believed that the poles reverse themselves on the average of once every million years. What causes this change? For a science fair project, draw and display a map showing the wandering of the poles over millions of years.

 **15**

Temporary

PROBLEM

How can you make a magnet by induction (magnetism produced when a magnetic material enters the field of a magnet)?

Materials

cardboard, about 1 foot (30 cm) square
thin book
index card
masking tape
bar magnet
box of BBs

Procedure

1. Place the edge of the cardboard on top of the book to form an incline.

2. Bend up about 1 inch (2.5 cm) of one short end of the index card.

3. Tape the card to the cardboard with the bent edge up and facing the book (see diagram).

4. Place the magnet on the cardboard, with the north pole facing the card. Move the magnet as close as possible without actually touching the index card.

5. Hold a BB against the upturned side of the index card. It should remain in position when released.

6. Touch the first BB with a second BB.

7. Continue adding BBs to the chain until the BBs no longer cling together.

8. Slowly move the magnet away from the chain of BBs.

Results

The number of BBs that cling together and hang down the incline will depend on the strength of the magnet. As soon as the magnet is moved away, the BBs pull away from each other and roll down the incline.

Why?

Every magnet is surrounded by a magnetic force field. The steel BBs, or any other magnetic materials, become magnets when placed in a magnetic field. Atoms act like tiny magnets with both a north and a south pole. When the magnetic material is placed near a magnet, the atoms in the magnetic material are pulled on by the magnet's force field, causing them to turn so that many of them point uniformly in the same direction.

The atoms in the first BB do not actually touch the magnet, but the magnetic force from the bar magnet enters the BB, causing the atoms to line up in the same direction as those in the magnet. The second and following BBs become magnetized in a similar way, but the force field comes from the magnetized BB it touches. Magnetism created in a magnetic material by touching or being near a magnet is called **induced magnetism**. The magnetic strength of the BBs depends on the strength of the magnetic field around the magnet and how close it is to the BBs. The force field from the bar magnet becomes weaker as the distance from the magnet increases. As the force field weakens, fewer atoms in the BBs line up. As a result, the BBs lose their magnetic power, pull away from each other, and roll down the incline.

LET'S EXPLORE

1. Would holding a different part of the magnet near the BBs affect the results? Repeat the experiment by first reversing the ends of the magnet, and then turning the magnet so that the side of the magnet is facing the index card. **Science Fair Hint:** Display diagrams showing the results of holding different parts of the magnet near the BBs.

2. Will other magnetic materials become temporarily magnetized by induction in the presence of a strong magnet? Repeat the original experiment using magnetic materials such as steel paper clips, thumbtacks, or pins. **Science Fair Hint:** Photographs and/or diagrams can be used to demonstrate **temporary magnets** (magnets that exhibit magnetic power only when touching, or placed near, a magnet) made from different materials.

SHOW TIME!

1. Another example of induced magnetism can be demonstrated by tying a small paper clip to a 12-inch (30-cm) piece of thread. Stack several books on a table. Place a bar magnet so that its end extends over the edge of the top book. Place the paper clip under the

end of the magnet, and slowly pull down on the string until the clip is suspended in the air. Tape the end of the string to the table, leaving the clip so that it appears to be floating in the air below the magnet. This model can be used as part of a project display.

2. Does the induced magnetic material retain any of its magnetic power? Touch an iron nail to a paper clip to test its lack of magnetic properties. Then hold a strong magnet near but not

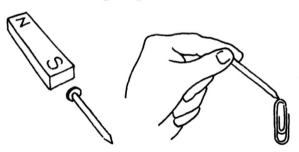

touching the nail. After three minutes, remove the magnet and touch the nail to the paper clip again. Diagrams showing the steps of this experiment can be included as part of a project display.

3. Design experiments to determine the answers to these questions about induced magnetism:

• Does the length of time the material remains near the magnet affect its magnetic powers?

• How does the shape of the material in which magnetism is being induced affect the results?

CHECK IT OUT!

Magnetic Resonance Images (MRI) are used to examine the soft, watery tissues of the human body, such as in the brain, gums, and internal organs. Your dentist or physician can help you to find out more about this magnetic testing, which has a magnetic field 30,000 times as strong as the earth's magnetic field. How important is the presence of water in the tissue being examined? What role does magnetic induction play in the forming of the magnetic images?

 **16**

Permanent

PROBLEM

How can you model a permanent magnet?

Materials

iron (steel) nail
paper clip
bar magnet

Procedure

1. Touch the nail to the paper clip to make sure they are not attracted to each other.

2. Lay the nail on a *wooden* table.

3. Hold the south-pole end of the magnet on top of the center of the nail.

4. With the south-pole end of the magnet, stroke the nail toward its point 30 times. Be sure to lift the magnet away from the nail when returning to the starting point for each stroke.

5. Touch the pointed end of the nail to the paper clip.

Results

The paper clip clings to the iron nail.

Why?

Iron and other magnetic materials act as if they have millions of tiny magnets inside them that point in different

directions. The correct name for a tiny magnet within a magnetic material is a domain. The bar magnet is a **permanent magnet** (a magnet that does not easily lose its magnetism). Stroking the nail with the bar magnet causes the domains inside the nail to line up. A permanent magnet can be made with this method, but most permanent magnets are made of mixtures of iron, nickel, cobalt, and other substances such as aluminum. The strength of any magnet depends on the number of domains that are lined up and facing the same way. A completely magnetized material has all of its domains facing in the same direction.

LET'S EXPLORE

1. Would stroking the nail with the north pole of the magnet affect the results? Repeat the experiment using the north pole of the magnet.

2. Would stroking the nail more times increase its magnetic strength? Repeat the original experiment twice, increasing the number of strokes. First stroke the nail 50 times on each end, and then try 75 strokes.

3. Would stroking the nail back and forth make a difference? Repeat the original experiment, but instead of lifting the magnet back to the starting point, drag the magnet back across the nail.

SHOW TIME!

How does rubbing a magnetic material with a magnet affect the polarity of the material? Repeat the original experiment to produce a magnetized nail. Tie a piece of thread to the center of the nail. Tape the free end of the thread to a pencil. Lay the pencil across the mouth of a glass jar so that the nail hangs freely inside the jar. Use a compass to determine which end of the nail is pointing north. From your results, write out a procedure so that the pointed end of one nail can be magnetized to become a north pole and the pointed end of a second nail can be magnetized to become a south pole.

CHECK IT OUT!

1. Iron, nickel, and cobalt are the only three metals that are attracted to a magnet. A mixture of any two or more metals is called an **alloy**. Mixtures combining one or more of the three

magnetic metals with other metals can produce a magnetic alloy if the percentage of magnetic material is high enough. Read about alloys of magnetic materials. Some things to discover in your research are:

- why a magnet is attracted to a Canadian nickel but not to a United States nickel.

- why the alloy called *alnico* is more magnetic than a natural iron magnet.

- what metals make up alnico and other magnetic alloys such as stainless steel and nichrome.

2. Find out how commercial magnets are made. A strong permanent magnet can be made by winding a coil of wire around a core of magnetic material, such as iron. An electric current is passed through the coil, which produces a magnetic field inside the coil. This magnetic field magnetizes the iron core by induction. (See Experiment 15 for an explanation of *induction*.) Find out more about using electricity to produce magnets. Is the strength of the magnet increased by an increase in current? Would the number of coils around the core affect the strength of the magnet produced?

 **17**

Attractive
Spirals

PROBLEM

What is an electromagnet?

Materials

box of BBs
saucer
2 inch × 3 feet (5 cm × 1 cm) strip of
　aluminum foil
1 new, clean penny
short, wide rubber band
long iron nail
D-cell battery

Procedure

1. Place 5 or 6 BBs in the saucer.

2. Fold the foil strip in half lengthwise
three times to form a thin strip that acts
like and will be called a wire.

3. Wrap the foil tightly around the nail.
Neatly overlap the layers leaving about
6 inches (15 cm) of free wire on each
end.

4. Wrap one end of the foil wire around
the penny. Tape the wrapped coin to
the negative battery terminal and the
second foil end to the positive terminal.
Stretch the rubber band around the
battery to hold the ends.

5. Holding the battery, touch the point of
the nail to a BB in the saucer.

6. Lift the nail.

7. Keep the ends of the wire on the battery poles, and try to pick up a chain of
BBs on the end of the nail. *WARNING:
In 10 seconds, or when the battery begins
to feel warm, remove the ends from the
battery poles.*

Results

A small chain of metal BBs clings to the end of the nail.

Why?

Electric currents can be used to produce a magnet. A magnetic field circles any wire carrying an electric current. Winding the foil into a coil (like a spring) pushes the magnetic field closer together and increases the strength of the magnet formed by the flowing electricity. Any coiled wire through which electricity flows is called a **solenoid**. The electric current flowing through the coils turns the wire into a magnet. Wrapping the foil around an iron nail produces a stronger magnet because the magnetism from the coils magnetizes the nail. The strength of the magnetism from the solenoid (coiled wire) and of the nail combine to produce a

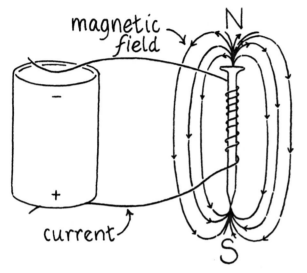

magnetic field

N

current

S

much stronger magnet. Magnets made by an electric current flowing through a wire are called **electromagnets**.

LET'S EXPLORE

1. Does the number of coils around the nail affect the strength of the electromagnet? Repeat the experiment twice, first by wrapping a longer length of foil around the nail, and then by replacing the long foil with a shorter length of foil. **Science Fair Hint:** Display the solenoids made with varying lengths of foil as part of a project display. Include

a short summary of the magnetic results of each test.

2. Does the size of the nail affect the strength of the electromagnet? Repeat the original experiment, first replacing the nail with a larger iron nail, and then using a smaller nail inside the solenoid. **Science Fair Hint:** Display photographs of the different-sized nails used inside the solenoid, showing the chain of BBs that each nail lifted.

3. How does the amount of electric current affect the strength of an electromagnet? Repeat the original experiment, but this time increase the electric current flowing through the solenoid by replacing the D-cell battery with two D-batteries. Tape the batteries together with the positive and negative ends touching. Attach the ends of the solenoid wire to the poles of the battery and hold the nail in your hand. *WARNING: Be sure to disconnect the wire from the battery when the nail begins to feel warm. It could get hot enough to burn your skin, and it drains the charge from the battery.* **Science Fair Hint:** Photographs and or drawings of the two electromagnets pro-

duced with D-cell and C-cell batteries can be displayed showing the number of BBs they can lift.

SHOW TIME!

Do the positive and negative ends of the battery affect the north and south magnetic poles on the electromagnet? Prepare an electromagnet as in the original experiment. Connect the foil to a battery, and hold the pointed end of the nail near a compass. *NOTE: Do not touch the nail to the compass, as it can change the polarity of the compass needle.* Reverse the solenoid so that the wire ends touch a different pole, and hold the point of the nail near the compass again. The pointed end of the magnetized nail is a south pole when it attracts the north end of the compass needle, but it is a north pole if it attracts the south end of the compass needle. Make drawings showing the connections of the solenoid wires and the magnetic poles produced as part of a project display.

CHECK IT OUT!

Huge electromagnets are used to pick up and transport cars at scrap yards. Read about electromagnets and find out about other uses for electromagnets. Select colorful magazine pictures of instruments containing electromagnets. Prepare a poster with these pictures that can be used as part of a project display.

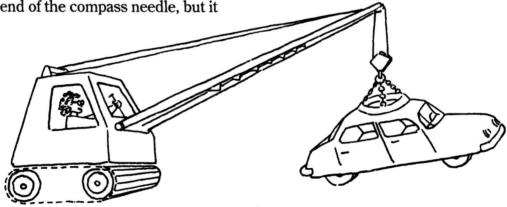

Demagnetize

PROBLEM

Does hitting a magnet weaken its magnetic strength?

Materials

iron nail
bar magnet
small paper clip
compass
wooden block
masking tape
adult helper
hammer

Procedure

NOTE: Never touch a compass with a magnet. Touching a compass with a strong magnet can change the polarity of the compass needle, causing the end marked north to become a south pole and all directions to be reversed.

1. Magnetize the nail by laying it on the magnet for three minutes.

2. Test the magnetic properties of the nail by touching it to the paper clip. The nail has been magnetized if the clip clings to it.

3. Lay the compass next to the wooden block.

4. Lay the magnetized nail on the wooden block so that the point of the nail faces east.

5. Tape the nail to the block.

6. Ask an adult to strike the nail 20 times with a hammer.

7. Test the magnetic properties of the nail again by touching it to the paper clip.

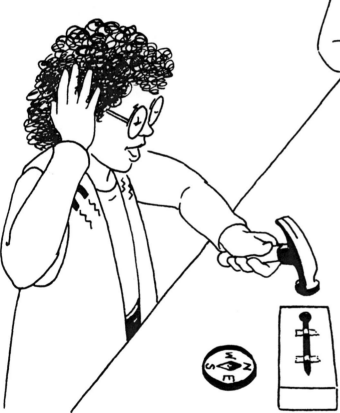

73

Results

The paper clip does not cling to the nail after the nail has been struck by the hammer.

Why?

Atoms within a magnet do not act individually, but combine to form groups called **domains**. Atoms within the domain act like tiny magnets and line up with their north ends pointing toward the earth's magnetic north pole. When many of these microscopic groupings of atomic magnets (domains) line up with their north poles in the same direction, a material becomes magnetic. Hitting the magnetized nail causes the orderly arrangement of the domains to be jarred out of place. The north poles randomly point in different directions. The nail loses its magnetic properties, and is said to be **demagnetized**. Turning the nail in an east-to-west direction prevents the domains from lining up with the earth's magnetic force field, which lies in a north-to-south direction.

LET'S EXPLORE

1. Does the nail have to be struck 20 times to demagnetize it? Repeat the

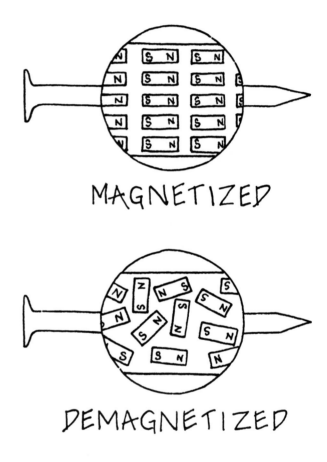

MAGNETIZED

DEMAGNETIZED

experiment, leaving the tip of the nail hanging over the edge of the wooden block so that it can be touched to a paper clip after each strike with the hammer. Record the least number of strikes required to demagnetize the nail. **Science Fair Hint:** Diagrams showing the position of domains before and after hitting the nail can be used as part of a project display.

2. Would laying the nail in a north-to-south direction affect its ease of being demagnetized? Repeat the original experiment, placing the nail in a north-to-south direction. Again place the tip of the nail over the edge of the wooden block, and touch it to a paper clip after each hammer strike. Compare the number of strikes to the number needed to demagnetize the nail in an east-to-west direction.

SHOW TIME!

Can you also demagnetize a nail by rubbing it back and forth with a magnet? Magnetize a nail and test its magnetism by touching it to a paper clip. Rub a magnet back and forth across the surface of the nail five or six times, and test the nail's magnetic properties again. Display a diagram showing the procedure of this experiment and indicate the results. Remember that demagnetized materials have domains pointing in random directions.

CHECK IT OUT!

Find out more about ways to reduce or destroy the magnetic properties of a magnet. Would cutting a magnet in half destroy it? How does heat affect magnetic properties? Do magnets lose their strength over periods of time?

 **19**

Pushing and Pulling

PROBLEM

Does placing magnets together always increase their combined magnetic attraction?

Materials

2 large sewing needles
bar magnet
scissors
ruler
sheet of paper
compass

Procedure

1. Lay the two sewing needles on top of the magnet, with the eye of each nee-

dle pointing toward the south pole of the magnet.

2. Allow the needles to remain on top of the magnet for at least one minute.

3. Remove the needles and insert the pointed ends through a piece of paper

measuring 4 inches × 4 inches (10 cm × 10 cm). The needles should be as close as possible and the ends even and pointing in the same direction.

4. Lay the compass on a *wooden* table, with the needle pointing toward the N printed on the compass face.

5. Hold the paper containing the two needles near the side of the compass marked with a W.

6. Observe any motion in the compass pointer.

7. Reverse the direction of one of the needles, so that the needles are close and the eyes point in opposite directions.

8. Again hold the paper containing the two needles near the side of the compass marked with a W, and observe any motion in the compass pointer.

Results

The compass pointer moves toward the ends of the sewing needles when their eyes are together. The compass pointer moves only slightly or not at all when the eyes of the needles are facing in opposite directions.

Why?

Placing the needles on the bar magnet causes the atoms in the needles to line up in a north-to-south direction. The needles become magnetized; their eyes become south poles, and their pointed ends become north poles. Laying the needles with their eyes pointing in the same direction puts the needles in a **parallel position** (with "like" poles together at each end). Both of the magnetized tips of the needles pull on the compass pointer. Combining the strengths of the two needle magnets in the parallel position produces a strong force on the compass pointer. Reversing the direction of one of the needles places the magnets in an **antiparallel position** (two "unlike" poles, a north pole and a south pole, together). Unlike poles work against each other; one is pushing while the other is pulling on the compass pointer. The result is the same as using a weak magnet or no magnet at all.

LET'S EXPLORE

1. Would laying the two sewing needles on top of a bar magnet with the eye of each needle pointing toward the north pole of the magnet affect the results? Repeat the experiment, this time positioning the needles so that the eyes both point toward the north end of the magnet.

2. Would other magnetized materials produce the same result? Repeat the original experiment using iron nails instead of needles. The nails could be held together instead of inserting them through a piece of paper.

SHOW TIME!

Use a pencil, three or four round magnets with a hole in the center, and iron filings to measure the strength of magnets in parallel and antiparallel positions. Place the pencil through the holes in the magnets. Support the bottom magnet while standing the point of the pencil in a mound of iron filings. Slowly lower the magnets until the iron filings begin to move. Perform the experiment with the "like" poles pointing in the opposite direction from each other. The repulsion between the magnets will cause them to float apart. Push the floating magnets together, or as close as possible, with your fingers and slowly slide them down the pencil toward the iron filings. Repeat the experiment with the magnets in an opposite position ("unlike" poles facing each other). The magnets will cling together and be easily lowered toward the filings. Diagrams and photographs of the experiment can be displayed. Display models by supporting the ends of the pencils in clay. Which is stronger? Why?

**20**

Eraser

PROBLEM

How do magnets affect recording tapes?

Materials

blank cassette tape
cassette recorder
strong magnet
pencil

Procedure

1. Place the cassette tape in the recorder.

2. Record your voice on the cassette tape. (Don't try this experiment with a tape you want to keep.)

3. Rewind the tape in the recorder and listen to your voice.

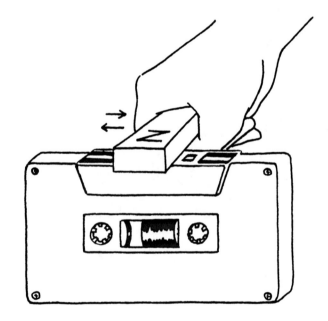

4. Remove the cassette from the recorder.

5. Use the pencil to rewind the cassette while rubbing the magnet against the tape as it appears. Continue until the beginning of the tape is reached.

6. Place the cassette tape back in the recorder and replay it.

7. Observe the sounds produced.

Results

Most or all of your voice will be erased.

Why?

The cassette tape contains a magnetic strip wound around two spools. Tiny magnetic particles are randomly scattered throughout the tape. The magnetic particles form no particular pattern on a blank tape. Sound waves entering the microphone of the machine are changed into electrical waves. These waves move magnets that are inside the machine, and the movement of the magnets rearranges the magnetic particles on the tape. Certain positions of the magnetic particles produce the sound of your voice. Rubbing the tape with a magnet causes the magnetic material to be pushed and pulled out of place. Rearranging the magnetic particles erases the sound of your voice. Magnetic recording tapes should be kept away from magnets.

LET'S EXPLORE

1. How close does the magnet have to be in order to affect the tape? Repeat the experiment, placing the magnet at different distances from the cassette ribbon. **Science Fair Hint:** Demonstrate the erasing of a voice from the cassette tape during an oral presentation of the project. Record someone's voice, play it back, and then use the magnet to erase the sound. Describe what the magnet is doing as you rub it across the tape.

2. Can different sounds be produced by the magnet? Move the magnet around on a blank tape in order to arrange the magnetic particles in different patterns. Experiment to determine if different movements of the magnet change the sound pattern on the tape. **Science Fair Hint:** Photographs taken of each step of the experiment can be displayed with brief descriptions of what is happening and the results.

SHOW TIME!

Would just laying a tape near a magnet affect the unexposed tape on the spools? Record your voice on a blank tape. Place a strong magnet and the tape in a box together. To allow enough time for any changes to occur, leave the materials in the box overnight. The next day, listen to the recording and determine the effect of the magnet on the unexposed magnetic tape.

CHECK IT OUT!

Valdemar Poulsen, a Danish engineer, was the first person to use wire to make magnetic sound recordings. Since Poulsen's time, wire has been replaced with magnetic tape. Read about the history of magnetic tape recordings. Questions to think about: How did Valdemar Poulsen's wire recordings work? What materials are used now to make recording tapes? How is a stereophonic tape different? How is sound recorded on the tape?

Glossary

Alloy A mixture of any two or more metals.

Antiparallel position Where unlike poles of magnets—a north pole and a south pole—are aligned.

Atom Smallest part of an element that retains the properties of the element.

Compass An instrument used to determine directions by means of a freely swinging magnetic needle which always points to the magnetic north.

Demagnetize To reduce or eliminate the magnetic properties of a magnet by causing the domains to be less uniform.

Dipolar Having a north and a south pole.

Dipping needle Instrument used to determine the patterns of a magnetic force field around a magnet. The needle is horizontal when the force lines are parallel to the earth, and dips downward in areas where the lines bend toward the earth.

Domain A cluster of atoms with their north poles pointing in the same direction.

Electromagnet A magnet produced by sending an electric current through a coil of wire.

Gravity The force that pulls things downward toward the earth's center.

Inclination Any deviation or change from a horizontal position.

Induced magnetism Magnetism caused by placing a magnet near or touching a magnetic material.

Magnetic Materials that have a uniform arrangement of their domains; the domains point in the same direction and are therefore attracted to magnets.

Magnetic equator The imaginary line between the north and south magnetic poles that divides the earth in half.

Magnetic field The pattern of magnetic lines of force around a magnet.

Magnetic monopoles Invisible particles believed by some scientists to fly out of the north pole of a magnet, loop around the magnet, and then fly back into the south pole of the magnet.

Magnetosphere The area of space around the earth affected by the earth's magnetic field.

Nonmagnetized Materials that have a haphazard arrangement of their domains; the domains point in many different directions, and are therefore not attracted to magnets.

Nonpermeable Materials that allow a magnetic force field to pass through without any disruptions in the magnetic field.

North pole The end of any magnet that is attracted toward the magnetic north pole of the earth.

Oscillation To swing back and forth one time.

Parallel position Where like poles of magnets are aligned.

Permanent magnet A magnet that retains its magnetic powers when not around another magnet.

Permeable Materials that gather in the magnetic lines of force, thereby disrupting the magnetic field.

Polarity A condition of having two different magnetic poles: one south pole and one north pole.

Solenoid A coil of wire through which electricity can flow.

South pole The end of any magnet that is attracted to the magnetic south pole of the earth.

Temporary magnet A magnet that exhibits magnetic powers only when touching or placed near a magnet.

Index